A SHORT STORY

THE STORY OF ZACCHAEUS

"Do not store up riches for yourselves here on earth for your heart will always be where your riches are." from Matthew 6:19-21

Written by Juli Foreman and Tricia Clem
Illustrated by Kevin Foreman

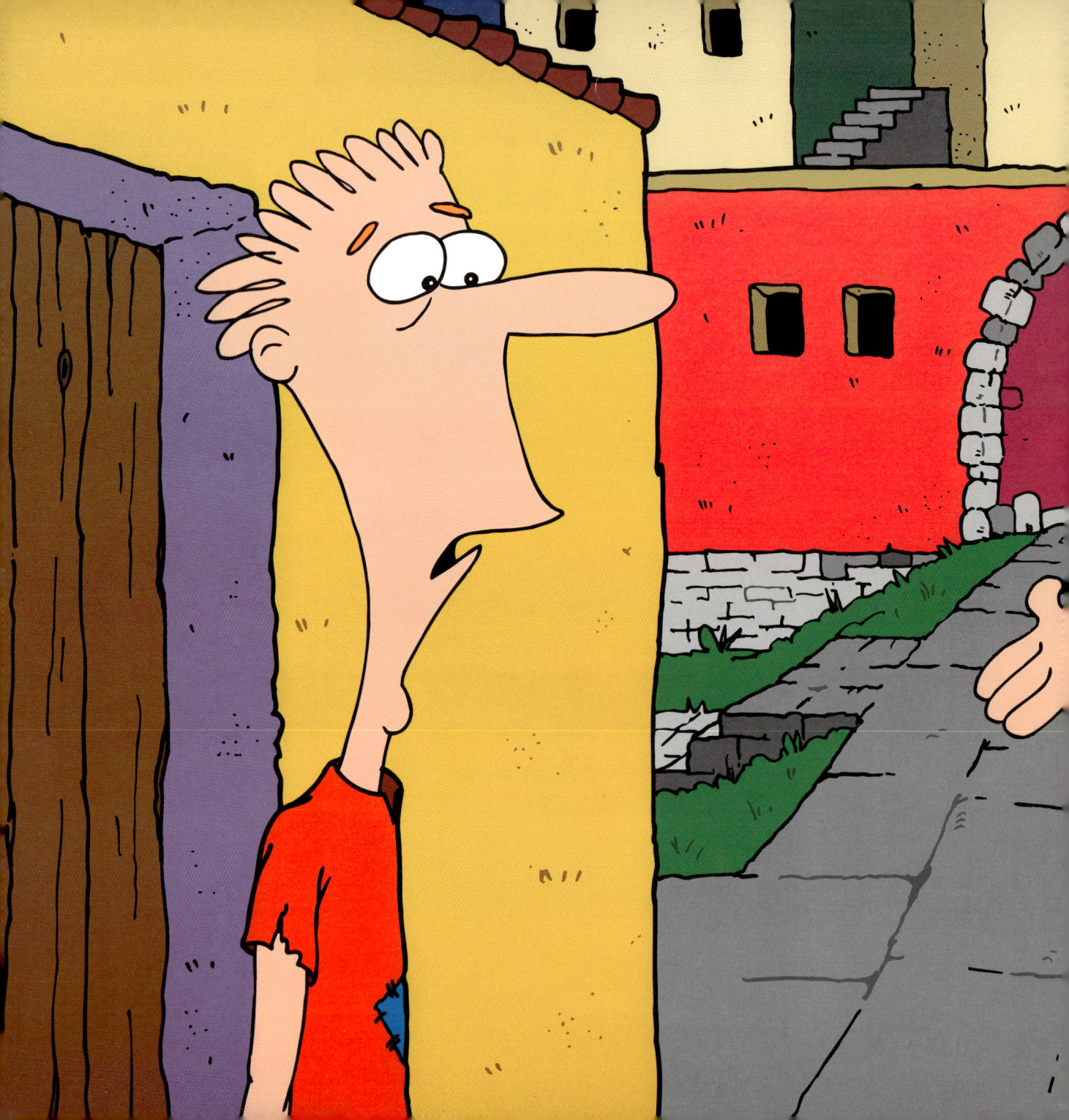

But, Zacchaeus had a problem. He was very short and the people in the crowd were too tall.

Zacchaeus had an idea. He ran ahead of the crowd and climbed a big tree. He said, "Now I am tall enough to see Jesus, too."

Jesus came by the tree and looked up.
He saw Zacchaeus out on a limb.

Zaccheaus climbed down very quickly. He was very excited. Jesus wanted to come to his house!

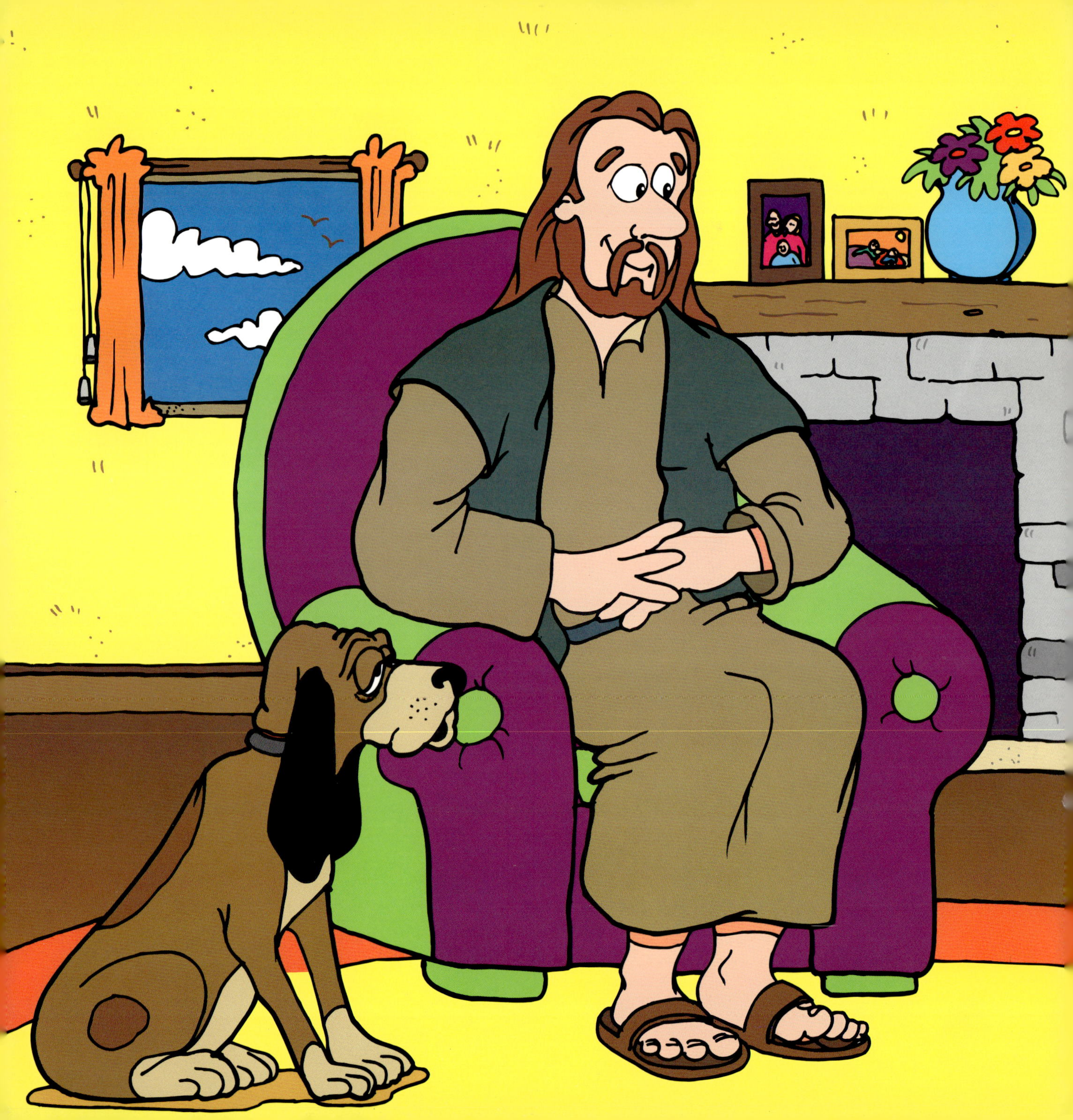

He told Jesus he would give half of all his money to people who were poor.

Zacchaeus also wanted to give back four times the money that he had unfairly taken.

Jesus was pleased with Zacchaeus. Jesus said, "Today you and your whole household have entered God's family." Just like Zacchaeus, we can also choose to do the right thing.